MASTERING EFFECTIVE COMMUNICATION FOR LEADERS

Unlocking The Secrets To Inspire And Engage Your Team

Nick Evans Brown

NICK EVANS BROWN

Copyright©2024 Nick Evans Brown

All Rights Reserve

YOU CAN GET ACCESS TO MORE BOOKS HERE:

OR

USING THE LINK BELOW:

https://amzn.to/3OvHJcr

MASTERING EFFECTIVE COMMUNICATION FOR LEADERS

TABLE OF CONTENTS

INTRODUCTION

CHAPTER ONE

1.0 THE FOUNDATIONS OF EFFECTIVE LEADERSHIP COMMUNICATION

1.1 THE ROLE OF TRANSPARENCY IN LEADERSHIP COMMUNICATION

1.2 STRATEGIES TO ENHANCE YOUR LISTENING SKILLS

1.3 HOW HONESTY PREVENTS MISUNDERSTANDINGS AND FOSTERS TRUST

CHAPTER TWO

2.0 NAVIGATING CHALLENGING CONVERSATIONS

2.1 TECHNIQUES FOR CONFLICT RESOLUTION

2.2 TECHNIQUES FOR SOLICITING INPUT FROM ALL TEAM MEMBERS

2.3 THE IMPACT OF OPEN DIALOGUE ON TEAM DYNAMICS AND PERFORMANCE

CHAPTER THREE

3.0 INSPIRING AND ENGAGING YOUR TEAM THROUGH EMPATHY

3.1 DISCUSSING THE BENEFITS OF EMPATHY ON TEAM RELATIONSHIPS AND OVERALL MORALE

3.2 IMPORTANCE OF RECOGNIZING AND CELEBRATING SUCCESSES

3.3 THE IMPACT OF PUBLIC RECOGNITION ON TEAM DYNAMICS

CONCLUSION

MASTERING EFFECTIVE COMMUNICATION FOR LEADERS

INTRODUCTION

"The art of communication is the language of leadership." - James Humes.

This strong sentence says it all about what it means to be a good leader in today's fast-paced world. Through "Mastering Effective Communication for Leaders: Unlocking the Secrets to Inspire and Engage Your Team," we explore the idea that good communication is more than just a skill; it's a vital tool that all leaders must master in order to motivate, inspire, and drive their teams to success.

Imagine going to a meeting where everyone is heard, ideas are shared easily, and working together is easy. This book will show you how to make that kind of setting. You will learn how to talk to your team in a way that is clear and makes sense, so your message gets through. We'll talk about the difficulties of having tough conversations

MASTERING EFFECTIVE COMMUNICATION FOR LEADERS

and find ways to turn them into chances for growth and understanding.

We'll also talk about how understanding can change the way leaders talk to people. When you get to know and connect with your team on a human level, you can build trust and loyalty, which will increase engagement and productivity.

This book has useful information and methods that you can use right away, no matter what level of experience you have as a manager or as a new leader. Each part is meant to give you the tools you need to improve your communication and leave an impression that lasts.

Join me on this trip to unlock the secrets of effective communication. Together, we will develop a leadership style that inspires your team and drives collective success. Let's begin!

CHAPTER ONE

1.0 The Foundations Of Effective Leadership Communication

Did you know that 70% of workers say they would work harder if they were better recognized? This statistic shows the important role effective communication plays in motivating and engaging employees. In "Mastering Effective Communication for Leaders: Unlocking the Secrets to Inspire and Engage Your Team," we will study the important components that form the backbone of effective leadership communication.

This chapter will focus on clarity and conciseness, two foundational elements that every leader must learn to inspire their teams and drive company success.

Clarity and Conciseness

MASTERING EFFECTIVE COMMUNICATION FOR LEADERS

Understanding The Importance Of Clear Messaging

Clear messaging is important for successful leadership communication. It ensures that team members understand their jobs, duties, and the organization's goals. When leaders speak clearly, they remove confusion and ambiguity, allowing their teams to align their efforts more effectively.

Alignment with Organizational Goals: Clear communication helps teams understand how their work adds to broader organizational goals. When workers grasp the goal and mission, they are more likely to feel connected to their work and motivated to help. For instance, a marketing team that knows how their campaigns align with the company's growth goals is more likely to innovate and push boundaries in their strategies.

Reduction of Misunderstandings: Ambiguity can lead to misinterpretations, which can result in mistakes, anger, and decreased morale. By articulating ideas clearly, leaders lessen the chances of misunderstandings that can derail projects. For example, if a project deadline is shared vaguely, team members may take it differently, leading to delays and missed targets.

Enhanced Decision-Making: When information is presented clearly, it helps team members to make informed decisions quickly. This agility is important in fast-paced settings where timely answers are necessary. Leaders who communicate standards empower their teams to take control of their tasks without constant oversight.

Techniques To Avoid Jargon And Ambiguity

While clarity is important, many leaders accidentally complicate their messages by using jargon or scientific language that may not be understood by

MASTERING EFFECTIVE COMMUNICATION FOR LEADERS

all team members. To generate clarity, leaders should adopt the following techniques:

Use Simple Language: Leaders should try to communicate in straightforward ways that everyone can understand. Instead of using industry-specific jargon or complex terminology, opt for plain language that sends your message effectively.

Example: Instead of saying, "We need to leverage our synergies," a boss might say, "Let's work together to improve our results." This simplification makes it easier for all team members to understand the idea without confusion.

Be Specific: Vague statements can lead to confusion about standards and duties. Leaders should provide specific knowledge about what they want from their teams.

Example: Instead of saying, "We need to improve our sales," a clearer message would be, "We need to increase our sales by 15% over the next quarter by targeting new customers." This detail gives team members a clear goal to aim for.

Break Down Complex Ideas: When discussing complex topics, leaders should break them down into manageable parts. Use bullet points or numbered lists to describe key ideas clearly.

Example: When introducing a new project, a leader might outline the goals, timelines, and individual duties in a clear list style. This structure helps team members digest information more easily.

Discovering How Clarity Fosters Trust And Alignment

Clarity in communication not only improves understanding but also promotes trust within teams. When leaders speak transparently and consistently, they build trust with their team members.

Building Trust Through Transparency: When leaders are clear about their intentions and standards, it creates an atmosphere of transparency where team members feel secure in expressing their thoughts and concerns. This trust supports open dialogue and cooperation.

Creating Alignment Through Consistency: Consistent messaging supports clarity and helps align team efforts with business goals. When leaders regularly share clear goals and updates, it ensures everyone is on the same page.

Encouraging Feedback: Clear communication welcomes comments from team members. When workers feel safe asking questions or seeking clarification, it leads to a more engaged workforce where everyone feels valued.

Practical Steps for Enhancing Clarity in Leadership Communication

To effectively apply clarity in communication, leaders can take several practical strategies:

Establish Clear Objectives: Before sharing any message, leaders should explain what they want to achieve with their communication. Establishing clear goals helps focus the message and ensures it connects with the audience.

Utilize Visual Aids: Incorporating visual aids such as charts, graphs, or slides can improve understanding by giving visual context for complex information. Visuals can help clarify key points and make information more accessible.

Encourage Questions: After giving a message, leaders should support team members to ask questions or seek clarification on any points that may be unclear. This practice not only reinforces clarity but also shows that the leader values feedback from their team.

Provide Written Summaries: After meetings or important talks, giving out written summaries can reinforce key points discussed while providing a reference for team members later on.

Practice Active Listening: Leaders should join in active listening during conversations with their teams. By showing genuine interest in what others have to say and reacting carefully, leaders can create an atmosphere where clarity thrives.

1.1 The Role Of Transparency In Leadership Communication

Transparency is a key aspect of successful leadership communication that supports clarity and conciseness. When leaders are open about business goals, challenges, and opportunities, they promote trust within their teams.

Fostering Trust Through Openness: Transparent communication helps employees to understand the bigger picture of organizational operations—what's working well and what isn't—creating an atmosphere of trust where employees feel empowered to share ideas and concerns without fear of retaliation.

Encouraging Collaboration: Open conversation encourages collaboration among team members as they feel safe sharing insights and ideas based on shared knowledge of organizational challenges and successes.

Addressing Concerns Promptly: Transparency helps address concerns before they escalate into bigger issues by inviting team members into talks about challenges faced by the company while encouraging collective problem-solving efforts.

In summary, clarity and conciseness are foundational aspects of successful leadership communication that significantly impact team dynamics and overall organizational success. By mastering these skills, leaders can ensure that their words resonate with team members while creating an environment of trust and collaboration.

MASTERING EFFECTIVE COMMUNICATION FOR LEADERS

As we move forward in this book, we will explore additional components of successful leadership communication—such as active listening and empathy—that further improve a leader's ability to inspire and engage their teams. Together, these factors create a robust framework for mastering effective communication in leadership roles—enabling you to unlock your team's full potential while driving your company toward success.

Remember that effective communication is not just about speaking; it's about building connections through clear messaging that inspires action—action that leads to recognition, engagement, and eventually greater productivity within your company. By prioritizing clarity in your communications as a leader, you set the stage for a thriving workplace where every employee feels valued and pushed to contribute their best efforts toward shared goals.

Active Listening

In "Mastering Effective Communication for Leaders: Unlocking the Secrets to Inspire and Engage Your Team," one of the most critical skills that leaders must develop is active listening. This skill is not merely about hearing what others say; it includes fully engaging with the speaker, getting their message, and responding thoughtfully. Active listening is important for building strong relationships, fostering collaboration, and making a positive work environment. In this chapter, we will explore the role of active listening in leadership, equip you with strategies to improve your listening skills and learn how to respond effectively to team feedback.

The Role Of Active Listening In Building Strong Relationships

Active listening plays a pivotal role in establishing and keeping strong relationships within a team. When leaders actively listen, they show respect and validation for their team members' thoughts and feelings. This practice creates an atmosphere of trust where employees feel valued and understood.

Creating a Safe Space: When leaders practice active listening, they create a safe space for open conversation. Employees are more likely to share their ideas, concerns, and feedback when they know their opinions will be heard without judgment. This openness promotes transparency and strengthens team cohesion.

Enhancing Emotional Intelligence: Active listening is a key component of emotional intelligence (EI). Leaders who actively listen are better able to understand the emotions and motivations of their team members. This understanding helps leaders to react appropriately to individual needs and concerns, thereby enhancing overall team dynamics.

Building Trust and Loyalty: Trust is essential in any relationship, especially in leadership. When leaders consistently show active listening, they build trust over time. Employees are more likely to remain loyal to leaders who value their input and show genuine interest in their views.

Facilitating Conflict Resolution: Active listening is particularly useful during conflicts or disagreements. By fully knowing different viewpoints before responding, leaders can mediate disputes more effectively. This method not only resolves conflicts but also reinforces relationships by showing that all parties are respected.

1.2 Strategies To Enhance Your Listening Skills

To become an effective active listener, leaders can adopt several practical strategies:

Undivided Attention: One of the most crucial elements of active listening is giving the speaker your full attention. This means reducing

MASTERING EFFECTIVE COMMUNICATION FOR LEADERS

distractions—such as phones or side conversations—and focusing solely on the person speaking. Make eye contact and use body language that expresses engagement.

Practice Tip: During conversations, consciously put away your phone or close your laptop to remove distractions. Show that you are present by nodding or using affirmational sounds like "uh-huh" or "I see."

Use Nonverbal Cues: Nonverbal communication plays a significant part in active listening. Your body language should show your attentiveness. Maintain eye contact, lean slightly forward, and use facial expressions that match the speaker's feelings.

Practice Tip: Pay attention to your own body language during talks. Ensure that it communicates interest and openness rather than disinterest or impatience.

Withhold Judgment: It's important to approach conversations with an open mind. Avoid forming judgments or responses while the other person is speaking; instead, focus on understanding their view fully.

Practice Tip: When you feel tempted to interrupt or critique while someone is speaking, take a deep breath and tell yourself that your goal is to understand first before responding.

Ask Open-Ended Questions: To expand your understanding of what the speaker is saying, ask open-ended questions that encourage them to elaborate on their thoughts.

Practice Tip: Instead of asking questions that can be answered with a simple "yes" or "no," try asking questions like "What do you think about…?" or "Can you tell me more about…?"

summarize and Summarize: After the speaker has finished sharing their thoughts, summarize what you heard to confirm your understanding. This method not only shows that you were listening but also allows the speaker to clarify any misunderstandings.

Practice Tip: Use sentences like "What I hear you saying is..." or "So you're suggesting that..." This technique reinforces your engagement in the talk.

Empathize with the Speaker: Empathy is a key component of careful listening. Try to put yourself in the speaker's shoes and understand their feelings and views.

Practice Tip: Reflect on how you would feel if you were in their position. Responding with empathy can help strengthen your relationship with the speaker.

Responding Effectively to Team Feedback

Once you have practiced active listening skills, it's equally important to react effectively to feedback from your team members. How leaders react can significantly impact team morale and engagement.

recognize Feedback: Always recognize the feedback given by team members, whether it's positive or constructive criticism. This acknowledgment shows that you value their opinion and encourages further communication.

Example Response: "Thank you for sharing your thoughts on this project; I appreciate your perspective."

Provide Constructive Responses: When addressing constructive comments, focus on solutions rather than dwelling on problems. Responding constructively helps create a collaborative environment where team members feel empowered to offer ideas for improvement.

Example Response: "I understand your concerns about our current process; let's brainstorm some solutions together."

MASTERING EFFECTIVE COMMUNICATION FOR LEADERS

Encourage Further Discussion: After responding to feedback, invite further discussion by asking additional questions or seeking clarification on specific points made by team members.

Example Response: "Can you elaborate on what aspects of our process you find most challenging? I'd love to hear more about your ideas."

Follow Up: If feedback leads to changes or actions taken within the team or company, follow up with those who provided input. Let them know how their feedback impacted decisions or improvements.

Example Response: "Thanks for your input last week; we implemented some changes based on your suggestions, and I'd love to hear how you think it's working."

Create an Open Feedback Culture: Encourage an ongoing culture of feedback within your team by regularly asking input from all members—not just during formal reviews but as part of everyday interactions.

Practice Tip: Use tools like anonymous surveys or suggestion boxes where workers can share their thoughts easily without fear of judgment.

The Impact of Active Listening on Team Dynamics

Active listening greatly enhances team dynamics by promoting open communication and collaboration:

Improved Collaboration: Teams that participate in active listening are more likely to collaborate effectively because members feel heard and valued for their contributions.

Increased Engagement: Employees who feel listened to are usually more engaged in their work because they perceive that their opinions count in decision-making processes.

MASTERING EFFECTIVE COMMUNICATION FOR LEADERS

Enhanced Problem-Solving: Active listening leads to better problem-solving as diverse viewpoints are considered before arriving at solutions.

Stronger Relationships: As trust builds through active listening techniques, relationships among team members strengthen, leading to a more cohesive work environment.

Positive Work Culture: A culture that values active listening promotes positivity within teams, encouraging innovation and creativity as employees feel safe sharing ideas without fear of dismissal.

Active listening is an important leadership skill that goes beyond mere hearing; it includes engaging fully with speakers, understanding their messages deeply, and responding thoughtfully. By practicing active listening techniques—such as giving undivided attention, using nonverbal cues, withholding judgment, asking open-ended questions, paraphrasing material, and empathizing with speakers—leaders can build stronger relationships with their teams.

Moreover, responding effectively to team comments creates an environment conducive to collaboration and innovation while fostering trust and loyalty among workers. As leaders cultivate these skills within themselves and support them among their teams, they will unlock new levels of engagement and productivity within their organizations.

In summary, learning active listening not only enhances individual leadership effectiveness but also transforms organizational culture into one where every voice matters—a vital step toward inspiring teams and driving collective success.

Transparency And Honesty

In "Mastering Effective Communication for Leaders: Unlocking the Secrets to Inspire and Engage Your Team," we dig into the important qualities of transparency and honesty in leadership communication. These qualities are not just ethical imperatives; they are foundational elements that promote trust, encourage open dialogue, and create a collaborative atmosphere where teams can grow. This chapter will explore the significance of openness in leadership communication, discuss how honesty can prevent misunderstandings nurture a culture of trust, and implement practices that promote open conversation and feedback within your team.

The Significance Of Transparency In Leadership Communication

Transparency in leadership refers to the openness with which leaders share information regarding their choices, tactics, and challenges. This freedom is important for several reasons:

Building Trust: Trust is the cornerstone of any successful team. When leaders speak transparently, they show integrity and reliability. Employees are more likely to trust leaders who freely share information about company goals, challenges, and changes. A transparent approach promotes a culture where team members feel safe to share their ideas and concerns without fear of retribution.

Example: A leader who shares both wins and setbacks during team meetings provides an environment where employees feel included in the organization's journey. This inclusion builds trust as workers see that their leaders are honest about the facts of the business.

Encouraging Engagement: Transparency encourages employee involvement by making team members feel valuable and involved in the decision-making process. When leaders share information about business performance or strategic shifts, workers are more likely to feel connected to the organization's goal.

Example: When a company is having financial challenges, a transparent leader will share this situation to their team rather than hiding it. By discussing possible solutions together, workers feel empowered to add ideas and solutions.

Facilitating Collaboration: Transparent communication supports teamwork among team members. When everyone has access to the same information, it reduces silos and helps collective problem-solving.

Example: In project management, if all team members are aware of each other's roles and challenges, they can collaborate more effectively to achieve shared goals.

Enhancing Accountability: Transparency holds leaders responsible for their actions and choices.

When leaders speak freely about their choices, they invite scrutiny and feedback from their teams. This accountability fosters a culture where everyone feels responsible for their contributions.

Example: If a leader commits to specific performance goals during a meeting, they set themselves up for accountability by publicly discussing progress toward those targets with their team.

1.3 How Honesty Prevents Misunderstandings And Fosters Trust

Honesty is another key component of successful leadership communication. It includes being truthful not only about wins but also about challenges and failures. Here's how honesty adds to successful communication:

Preventing Misunderstandings: Honest communication helps clarify norms and reduces ambiguity. When leaders are straightforward about

MASTERING EFFECTIVE COMMUNICATION FOR LEADERS

what they expect from their teams, it lowers the chances of misinterpretation.

Example: Instead of saying, "We need to improve our customer service," a leader could specify, "We need to reduce customer response times by 20% over the next quarter." This clarity stops misunderstandings about what is needed.

Fostering Open Dialogue: Honesty promotes an open dialogue between leaders and team members. When leaders practice honesty by sharing their thoughts candidly, it sets a precedent for others to do the same. Example: A leader who admits when they don't have all the answers asks team members to share their thoughts without fear of judgment. This openness offers an environment where diverse ideas can be shared freely.

Building Emotional Safety: When leaders are honest about challenges or mistakes, it offers emotional safety within the team. Employees feel more comfortable admitting their own mistakes or asking for help when they know their boss is also willing to be vulnerable.

Example: A leader who shares a past failure in a project can encourage team members to talk their challenges without fear of negative consequences.

Strengthening Relationships: Honesty improves relationships between leaders and workers by fostering mutual respect. When workers see that their leaders are genuine in their communications, it improves loyalty and commitment.

Example: Leaders who provide constructive comments honestly while also recognizing successes reinforce good relationships with their teams.

Implementing Practices That Promote Open Dialogue and Feedback

MASTERING EFFECTIVE COMMUNICATION FOR LEADERS

To cultivate transparency and honesty within your company, leaders should adopt specific practices that promote open dialogue and encourage feedback:

Establish Regular Check-Ins: Schedule regular one-on-one meetings with team members to discuss progress, challenges, and feedback openly. These meetings offer chances for honest conversations about performance expectations and personal growth.

Practice Tip: Use these check-ins not only to provide feedback but also to solicit input from workers about how they feel regarding their jobs or any obstacles they face.

Encourage Anonymous Feedback: Create channels for anonymous feedback where workers can share concerns or ideas without fear of backlash. This practice supports honesty while allowing leaders to gain insight into areas that may need improvement.

Practice Tip: Use online survey tools or suggestion boxes where workers can give feedback anonymously on various parts of the workplace culture or leadership practices.

Model Vulnerability as a Leader: Share your own experiences—both wins and failures—with your team. By being open about your journey as a leader, you encourage others to do the same.

Practice Tip: During team meetings or company-wide events, take time to share lessons learned from specific challenges you've faced as a leader.

Create an Open-Door Policy: Encourage an open-door policy where workers feel safe approaching you with questions or concerns at any time. Being accessible supports an environment where open dialogue is prioritized.

MASTERING EFFECTIVE COMMUNICATION FOR LEADERS

Practice Tip: Make it clear that you welcome questions or talks at any time by regularly telling your team that your door is always open for them.

Celebrate Transparency in Team Culture: Recognize people or teams who exhibit transparency in their communication practices. Celebrating these behaviors promotes the value of honesty within your organization's culture.

Practice Tip: During team meetings or company events, highlight examples of open communication among peers as best practices worth following.

Provide Training on Effective Communication: Offer training workshops focused on improving conversation skills among all employees—especially around transparency and honesty in interactions.

Practice Tip: Organize workshops that cover themes like active listening, giving constructive comments, and fostering open dialogue within teams.

Transparency and honesty are foundational elements of effective leadership communication that significantly impact business culture and employee engagement. By embracing transparency in sharing information about goals, obstacles, and successes, leaders build trust among their teams while encouraging collaboration and responsibility.

Honesty avoids misunderstandings by clarifying standards while supporting open dialogue that strengthens relationships within teams. Implementing practices such as regular check-ins, anonymous feedback channels, modeling vulnerability, keeping an open-door policy, celebrating transparency in culture, and offering training on effective communication will further enhance these qualities within your company.

MASTERING EFFECTIVE COMMUNICATION FOR LEADERS

As you develop openness and honesty as core values in your leadership approach, you will create an environment where trust flourishes—empowering your teams to engage fully with their work while driving collective success toward shared goals. In this way, you not only enhance your effectiveness as a leader but also encourage those around you to accept these principles in their interactions—ultimately leading to a thriving organizational culture built on mutual respect and collaboration.

CHAPTER TWO

2.0 Navigating Challenging Conversations

Research shows that leaders who participate in difficult talks can improve team performance by up to 25%. This striking figure underscores the importance of effectively navigating challenging talks in leadership. In "Mastering Effective Communication for Leaders: Unlocking the Secrets to Inspire and Engage Your Team," we will explore methods for addressing tough topics while keeping team morale. This chapter will focus on preparing for difficult conversations, including finding the right time and place, equipping yourself with tools for constructive framing, and building a solution-focused mindset.

Preparing For Difficult Discussions.

Identifying the Right Time and Place.

MASTERING EFFECTIVE COMMUNICATION FOR LEADERS

The timing and setting of a challenging talk can greatly impact its outcome. Leaders must be intentional about choosing when and where to join in these talks.

Choose an Appropriate Environment: The physical setting can influence how comfortable people feel during a difficult talk. Opt for a private place where both parties can speak openly without interruptions or distractions. Avoid public areas or places where others might overhear sensitive talks.

Example: If you need to handle performance problems with a team member, find a quiet meeting room rather than discussing it in a bustling office or during a team meeting.

Timing Matters: Timing is crucial when approaching challenging topics. Consider the emotional state of the people involved, as well as any pressing deadlines or stressors they may be facing. Choose a moment when both sides are likely to be calm and focused.

Example: Avoid initiating a difficult talk right before a big deadline or during stressful times. Instead, schedule a time when both you and the team member can engage thoughtfully.

Set Clear Objectives: Before the talk, clarify your goals. What do you hope to achieve? Are you trying to settle a conflict, provide feedback, or address a performance issue? Having clear goals will guide the talk and help keep it on track.

Practice Tip: Write down your goals before the meeting so you can refer back to them during the conversation if needed.

Equipping Yourself with Tools for Framing Issues Constructively

The way leaders approach issues significantly affects how they are viewed by team members.

MASTERING EFFECTIVE COMMUNICATION FOR LEADERS

Constructive framing supports open dialogue and cooperation rather than defensiveness.

Use "I" Statements: Frame your worries using "I" statements to describe your feelings without placing blame. This way helps convey your perspective while minimizing defensiveness from the other party.

Example: Instead of saying, "You never meet deadlines," try saying, "I feel concerned when deadlines are missed because it impacts our project timeline." This way focuses on your feelings rather than accusing the other person.

Focus on Specific Behaviors: When discussing problems, focus on specific behaviors rather than making generalizations about the person's character. This method helps keep the conversation objective and focused on actionable changes.

Example: Rather than saying, "You're not a team player," specify, "I noticed that during our last project meeting, you didn't contribute to the discussion." This specificity allows for constructive feedback.

Highlight Impact: Explain how the behavior in question affects the team or company. By illustrating the consequences of actions, you build a context for why the talk is important.

Example: You might say, "When reports are submitted late, it delays our ability to make informed decisions as a team." This framing helps the individual understand why their deeds count.

Encourage Dialogue: Invite the other person to share their view throughout the talk. This method fosters collaboration and shows that you value their opinion.

Practice Tip: Use open-ended questions such as "Can you help me understand your thought process?" or "What challenges are you facing that we should discuss?" This encourages engagement and dialogue.

Developing a Mindset Focused on Solutions Rather Than Problems

A solution-focused mindset is important when navigating challenging talks. Rather than dwelling on problems, leaders should try to collaboratively explore answers with their team members.

Shift from Blame to Solutions: Instead of assigning blame for problems, focus on identifying answers together. A collaborative approach allows team members to take ownership of their actions and contribute to problem-solving efforts.

Example: If an employee consistently misses deadlines, instead of saying, "You need to do better," ask, "What can we do together to ensure deadlines are met moving forward?" This welcomes collaboration and ownership of answers.

Encourage Brainstorming: During discussions, ask team members to brainstorm possible solutions or strategies for improvement. This practice supports creativity and engagement while reinforcing that everyone has a role in finding solutions.

Practice Tip: Use questions like "What ideas do you have for overcoming this challenge?" or "How can we work together to improve this situation?" These questions promote active participation in problem-solving.

Be Open to comments: Encourage comments from team members about your leading style or communication methods as well. This openness shows humility and reinforces that everyone is part of the answer process.

Example: After discussing an issue, ask, "How can I support you better in this area?" This question

MASTERING EFFECTIVE COMMUNICATION FOR LEADERS

welcomes discussion about your role in facilitating success.

Follow Up on Progress: After addressing challenging topics, plan follow-up meetings to assess progress toward agreed-upon answers. Regular check-ins show commitment to growth and accountability for both parties involved.

Practice Tip: Set exact dates for follow-up meetings during your initial talk so that everyone knows when they will reconvene to discuss progress.

Navigating challenging conversations is an important skill for successful leadership communication that can greatly enhance team performance and morale. By preparing thoughtfully—choosing appropriate times and places for discussions, framing problems constructively, and adopting a solution-focused mindset—leaders can handle tough topics while creating an environment of trust and collaboration within their teams.

As we continue through "Mastering Effective Communication for Leaders," remember that engaging in tough talks is not merely about addressing problems; it's about empowering your team members and building pathways toward growth and improvement. By implementing these strategies successfully, you will not only enhance your leadership effectiveness but also inspire those around you to embrace open conversation as a vital component of organizational success.

2.1 Techniques For Conflict Resolution

In "Mastering Effective Communication for Leaders: Unlocking the Secrets to Inspire and Engage Your Team," we explore the important role of conflict resolution poor leadership. Research shows that leaders who participate in difficult talks can improve team performance by up to 25%. This chapter will delve into essential communication techniques used

MASTERING EFFECTIVE COMMUNICATION FOR LEADERS

by top leaders to mediate conflicts, explore methods for building a collaborative atmosphere during disagreements, and implement actionable steps to turn conflicts into opportunities for growth.

Discovering Essential Communication Techniques Used by Top Leaders

Effective dispute resolution starts with strong communication skills. Leaders must employ various methods to mediate disputes successfully and guide their teams toward resolution.

Active Listening: One of the most important skills in dispute resolution is active listening. This includes giving full attention to the speaker, understanding their viewpoint, and acknowledging their feelings. Active listening helps de-escalate tensions and provides a sense of validation.

Technique: Use open body language, keep eye contact, and nod to show interest. Paraphrase what the other person has said to confirm understanding. For example, "What I hear you saying is that you feel overwhelmed by the project deadlines."

Establishing Ground Rules: Before engaging in a conflict resolution discussion, it's important to set ground rules that support respectful communication. This includes agreeing on how each party will share their views and ensuring that everyone has a fair chance to speak.

Technique: At the beginning of the talk, outline rules such as "No interrupting" and "Focus on issues, not personal attacks." This makes a safe setting for open dialogue.

Using "I" Statements: When talking grievances, leaders should frame their worries using "I" statements rather than "you" statements. This way reduces defensiveness and focuses on the speaker's feelings rather than blaming others.

MASTERING EFFECTIVE COMMUNICATION FOR LEADERS

Technique: Instead of saying, "You never listen to my ideas," try saying, "I feel frustrated when my ideas aren't acknowledged during meetings." This moves the attention from blame to personal experience.

Clarifying Misunderstandings: Often, disputes emerge from misunderstandings or miscommunications. Leaders should take time to clarify any points of confusion before continuing with answers.

Technique: Ask detailed questions like, "Can you explain what you meant by that?" or "I'm not sure I fully understand your perspective; could you elaborate?" This encourages dialogue and ensures all groups are on the same page.

Focusing on Solutions: Rather than dwelling on problems or assigning blame, successful leaders guide discussions toward finding answers. This proactive method fosters collaboration and pushes teams to work together toward common goals.

Technique: After identifying the issues at hand, ask questions like, "What can we do together to resolve this?" or "What solutions can we brainstorm that would satisfy everyone involved?"

Exploring Methods For Fostering A Collaborative Atmosphere During Disagreements

Creating a collaborative environment during disagreements is important for successful conflict resolution. Leaders can take several strategies to foster collaboration:

Encouraging Open Dialogue: Leaders should support an atmosphere where team members feel safe expressing their thoughts and feelings without fear of retribution. Encouraging open dialogue helps build trust and allows more effective discussions.

Technique: Regularly check in with team members about their thoughts on ongoing projects or team dynamics. Use team meetings as platforms for sharing problems openly.

Finding similar Ground: In many conflicts, both sides share similar goals or values that can serve as a foundation for resolution. Identifying these commonalities can help shift focus away from differences and toward collaboration.

Technique: During discussions, ask questions like, "What do we all want to achieve here?" or "How can we align our goals to find a solution?" This drives participants to see themselves as part of a unified team rather than adversaries.

Brainstorming Solutions Together: Collaborative problem-solving includes brainstorming possible answers as a team rather than imposing decisions from above. This method empowers team members and promotes a sense of ownership over the resolution process.

Technique: Facilitate brainstorming meetings where all ideas are accepted without judgment. Use techniques like mind mapping or group discussions to build creative solutions collectively.

Utilizing Mediation Techniques: In more complex battles, leaders may need to act as mediators between conflicting groups. Mediation involves facilitating talks between parties while staying neutral and focused on finding mutually acceptable solutions.

Technique: As a mediator, encourage each party to share their views while ensuring that both sides listen carefully. Summarize key points made by each party to clarify knowledge before moving forward with possible solutions.

Maintaining a Positive Attitude: A positive attitude can greatly influence the tone of conflict resolution talks. Leaders should model positivity and optimism throughout the process, reinforcing that goals are doable.

Technique: Use positive language and affirmations during discussions, such as "I believe we can find a solution together" or "Let's focus on what we can achieve moving forward."

Implementing Actionable Steps to Turn Conflicts into Opportunities for Growth

Conflicts do not have to end negatively; they can be turned into chances for growth and improvement within teams. Here are real steps leaders can take:

Acknowledge Conflict Early: Address conflicts quickly before they escalate into bigger issues. Early intervention shows proactive leadership and prevents resentment from building among team members.

Action Step: Regularly assess team dynamics through informal check-ins or surveys to spot possible conflicts early on.

Conduct Root Cause Analysis: When conflicts appear, take time to analyze underlying causes rather than just treating surface-level symptoms. Understanding root causes helps leaders to adopt lasting solutions that prevent future problems.

Action Step: Use tools like the "5 Whys" technique—asking why multiple times until reaching the core issue—to find underlying problems contributing to conflict.

Create Development Plans Post-Conflict: After resolving conflicts, work with involved parties to build action plans aimed at preventing similar problems in the future. These plans should describe specific steps each party will take going forward.

Action Step: Schedule follow-up meetings after resolving conflicts to review work on action plans and talk any leftover concerns or challenges.

Encourage Continuous Learning: Promote a mindset of continuous learning within your team by encouraging people to think on conflicts as learning events rather than failures.

Action Step: After resolving a disagreement, hold a debrief session where team members share insights learned from the experience and discuss how they can apply these lessons in future interactions.

Celebrate Successful Resolutions: Recognizing successful conflict resolutions reinforces good habits within your team. Celebrating these moments motivates others to participate positively in future disagreements.

Action Step: Acknowledge individuals who helped positively during conflict resolution processes in team meetings or through internal messaging.

Navigating conflict is an inevitable part of leadership that offers both challenges and chances for growth within teams. By employing important communication techniques—such as active listening, setting ground rules, using "I" statements, clarifying misunderstandings, and focusing on solutions—leaders can successfully mediate conflicts while fostering collaboration among team members.

Creating an environment that supports open conversation, finds common ground, utilizes mediation techniques, keeps a positive attitude, and transforms conflicts into opportunities for growth will enhance total team dynamics and performance.

As you continue your journey through "Mastering Effective Communication for Leaders," remember

MASTERING EFFECTIVE COMMUNICATION FOR LEADERS

that effectively managing conflict is not merely about resolving disputes but about cultivating relationships built on trust and collaboration—ultimately leading your organization toward greater success through collective effort and shared understanding.

Encouraging Open Dialogue

In "Mastering Effective Communication for Leaders: Unlocking the Secrets to Inspire and Engage Your Team," one of the most important components of successful leadership is creating an environment of open conversation. Research suggests that leaders who support open communication can significantly enhance team dynamics, leading to improved performance and collaboration. This chapter will explore how to create a safe environment for team members to share concerns, techniques for soliciting input from all team members regardless of hierarchy, and the impact of open dialogue on team dynamics and performance.

Creating a Safe Environment for Expression

Creating a safe space for open dialogue is essential for encouraging team members to share their thoughts, concerns, and ideas without fear of retribution or criticism. Here are several ways leaders can use to foster this environment:

Establish Psychological Safety: Psychological safety refers to a climate in which people feel okay taking interpersonal risks. Leaders must communicate that it is okay to share ideas, ask questions, and voice worries without fear of negative consequences.

Action Step: Begin meetings by affirming that all contributions are valued and that differing ideas are welcome. For example, you might say, "I want everyone to feel comfortable sharing their thoughts today, even if they differ from mine."

MASTERING EFFECTIVE COMMUNICATION FOR LEADERS

Model Vulnerability: Leaders who model vulnerability by sharing their challenges and mistakes create an atmosphere where team members feel safe to do the same. This openness promotes trust and encourages others to share their stories.

Action Step: Share a personal story about a problem you faced and what you learned from it. This sets the tone for authenticity and motivates others to share their own stories.

Encourage Active Participation: Actively invite feedback from all team members during discussions. This can be done by directly asking quieter members for their opinion or using structured forms that give everyone a chance to speak.

Action Step: Use round-robin forms during talks where each person gets a turn to share their thoughts. This means that everyone has a chance to contribute.

Provide Constructive Feedback: When team members share concerns or ideas, react with constructive feedback that acknowledges their contributions while guiding them toward growth.

Action Step: Use phrases like "That's an interesting perspective; let's explore it further" or "I appreciate your honesty; here's how we might address this issue together." This reinforces that feedback is part of growth.

Celebrate Contributions: Recognizing and celebrating efforts from team members reinforces the worth of open conversation. When employees see their view acknowledged, they are more likely to engage in future discussions.

Action Step: Publicly acknowledge efforts during meetings or through internal messages, such as newsletters or team updates.

2.2 Techniques For Soliciting Input From All Team Members

To ensure that all views are heard, leaders must actively solicit input from every team member, regardless of their position within the hierarchy. Here are effective ways for achieving this:

Use Anonymous Feedback Tools: Implement anonymous polls or idea boxes where team members can share their thoughts without fear of identification. Anonymity can spur more honest comments.

Action Step: Utilize online tools like Google Forms or SurveyMonkey to create anonymous surveys after meetings or project completions to gather thoughts on team dynamics and areas for growth.

Hold Regular Check-Ins: Schedule regular one-on-one check-ins with team members to share their thoughts on projects, challenges they face, and any ideas they may have for improvement.

Action Step: During these check-ins, ask open-ended questions like "What challenges are you currently facing?" or "Do you have any suggestions for how we can improve our processes?"

Encourage Peer-to-Peer Feedback: Foster a system where team members provide feedback to one another in addition to getting feedback from leaders. This method supports collaboration and mutual respect among colleagues.

Action Step: Implement peer review sessions where team members can give helpful feedback on each other's work in a structured format, ensuring everyone has a chance to participate.

Utilize Brainstorming Sessions: Organize brainstorming meetings especially meant for generating ideas on projects or addressing challenges. Encourage all participants to share without judgment during these meetings.

Action Step: Use methods like mind mapping or sticky note tasks where everyone writes down ideas anonymously before discussing them as a group.

Create Cross-Functional Teams: Form cross-functional teams that bring together people from different departments or roles within the company. This diversity encourages varied views and improves collaboration.

Action Step: Assign projects that require input from various functions within the company, allowing people to collaborate and share insights based on their unique expertise.

2.3 The Impact Of Open Dialogue On Team Dynamics And Performance

Open dialogue has profound effects on team dynamics and total success within a business. Here are some key impacts:

Enhanced Trust Among Team Members: When team members feel safe expressing themselves freely, it fosters trust within the group. Trust leads to stronger ties and encourages collaboration among people.

Impact Analysis: A study run by Gallup found that teams with high levels of trust experience 21% higher productivity compared to those with lower trust levels. Open discussion builds this trust by allowing individuals to share vulnerabilities without fear.

Improved Problem-Solving Abilities: Open communication enables the sharing of diverse views, which enhances problem-solving capabilities within teams. When everyone adds their thoughts, teams can analyze challenges more thoroughly and create innovative solutions.

Impact Analysis: Research shows that teams that value communication beat their peers by 50%. This

MASTERING EFFECTIVE COMMUNICATION FOR LEADERS

statistic shows how effective dialogue leads to better decision-making and problem-solving results.

Increased Engagement and Morale: Teams that practice open dialogue tend to have better levels of engagement and morale among workers. When people feel heard and valued, they are more likely to be motivated in their jobs.

Impact Analysis: According to a study by Gallup, organizations with high employee engagement experience 21% higher income than those with disengaged employees—demonstrating how open communication adds directly to business success.

Fostering Innovation: Open dialogue promotes creativity by allowing individuals to easily share new ideas without fear of criticism. This culture of innovation leads teams to try new approaches and answers successfully.

Impact Analysis: Organizations that promote inclusive communication report a 19% increase in team performance due to enhanced creativity coming from diverse views being shared freely.

Conflict Resolution Improvement: When open dialogue is encouraged, conflicts can be handled more constructively before they escalate into bigger issues. Team members who speak openly are better able to settle disagreements amicably.

Impact Analysis: A study by the Institute for Corporate Productivity found that teams with strong communication practices experience 30% fewer conflicts than those with bad communication structures—highlighting how open dialogue helps in conflict management.

Encouraging open dialogue is important for successful leadership communication in any company. By creating an environment where team members feel safe voicing their concerns,

MASTERING EFFECTIVE COMMUNICATION FOR LEADERS

employing techniques for soliciting input regardless of hierarchy, and understanding the effect of open conversation on team dynamics and performance, leaders can support collaboration and innovation within their teams.

As you continue your journey through "Mastering Effective Communication for Leaders," remember that promoting open dialogue is not just about improving communication; it's about building a culture where every voice matters—a culture that drives engagement enhances problem-solving capabilities, fosters trust among colleagues, and ultimately leads organizations toward greater success through collective effort and shared understanding.

CHAPTER THREE

3.0 Inspiring And Engaging Your Team Through Empathy

Studies show that empathetic leaders have teams with 50% higher participation levels. This compelling figure shows the transformative power of empathy in leadership communication. In "Mastering Effective Communication for Leaders: Unlocking the Secrets to Inspire and Engage Your Team," we will study how empathy serves as a cornerstone for successful leadership, improving team dynamics, morale, and overall performance. This chapter will define empathy, talk its part in effective communication, explore how empathetic communication can revolutionize your leadership approach, and highlight the benefits of empathy on team relationships.

MASTERING EFFECTIVE COMMUNICATION FOR LEADERS

Understanding Empathy In Leadership

Defining Empathy

Empathy is the ability to understand and share the thoughts of another person. It goes beyond mere sympathy; empathy includes stepping into someone else's shoes and genuinely comprehending their viewpoint, emotions, and experiences. In a leadership setting, empathy means recognizing and responding to the feelings of peers, subordinates, and superiors.

Empathy can be broken down into three key components:

Cognitive Empathy: The ability to understand another person's position or mental state. This includes understanding their thoughts and feelings without necessarily sharing those emotions.

Emotional Empathy: The ability to physically feel what another person is feeling. This emotional connection helps leaders to connect on a deeper level with their team members.

Compassionate Empathy: This goes a step further by not only understanding and feeling but also being moved to help or support others based on that understanding.

The Role Of Empathy In Effective Communication

Empathy plays a crucial part in effective communication by creating an environment where team members feel understood and valued. When leaders communicate with empathy, they create a safe place for open dialogue, which is important for collaboration and innovation.

Building Trust: Empathetic talk builds trust between leaders and team members. When employees feel

MASTERING EFFECTIVE COMMUNICATION FOR LEADERS

that their leaders truly care about their well-being, they are more likely to interact openly and honestly.

Enhancing Understanding: By practicing empathy, leaders can better understand the challenges and motivations of their team members. This understanding helps them to tailor their communication style to meet the needs of individuals successfully.

Facilitating Conflict Resolution: Empathy equips leaders with the tools needed to handle disagreements constructively. By understanding the feelings underlying disagreements, empathetic leaders can mediate successfully and help find common ground.

Encouraging Feedback: When leaders show empathy, team members feel more comfortable giving feedback or expressing worries. This open sharing of ideas leads to continuous growth within the team.

Exploring How Empathetic Communication Can Revolutionize Your Leadership Approach

Empathetic conversation can fundamentally change how leaders connect with their teams. Here are several ways it can change your leading approach:

Creating a Culture of Openness: Leaders who communicate empathetically create a culture where team members feel safe sharing their ideas without fear of judgment or reprisal. This openness encourages creativity and innovation as workers feel empowered to add ideas.

Example: A leader who actively seeks input during meetings by asking for diverse perspectives shows an empathetic approach that values each team member's voice.

Enhancing Employee Engagement: When workers feel understood and valued through empathetic interactions, they are more likely to be involved in their job. Engaged workers are more productive, motivated, and committed to meeting company goals.

Research Insight: According to Gallup, businesses with high employee engagement levels experience 21% higher profitability compared to those with low engagement levels.

Fostering Resilience: Empathetic leaders help build resilience within their teams by giving emotional support during difficult times. When employees know they have a leader who gets their struggles, they are better able to cope with stressors.

Example: During times of high workload or tight deadlines, an empathetic leader might check in with team members individually to give support or adjust expectations based on individual circumstances.

Improving Retention Rates: Employees who feel appreciated and supported by empathetic leaders are less likely to leave the business. High retention rates save companies time and resources involved with hiring and training new hires.

Research Insight: A study by CJPI found that organizations run by empathetic leaders see better morale and lower turnover rates due to enhanced employee satisfaction.

Encouraging Collaboration: Empathetic communication promotes collaboration among team members by building an environment where individuals feel comfortable sharing ideas and working together toward shared goals.

Example: An empathetic leader might support brainstorming sessions where all team members are encouraged to add ideas without fear of criticism.

3.1 Discussing The Benefits Of Empathy On Team Relationships And Overall Morale

The benefits of empathy stretch beyond individual interactions; they significantly impact team relationships and general morale within an organization:

Strengthening Relationships: Empathy fosters strong relationships among team members by forming ties built on trust and understanding. When people feel linked to one another, collaboration becomes more natural.

Impact Analysis: Research shows that teams characterized by strong interpersonal relationships are more cohesive and perform better than those missing these ties.

Boosting Morale: A workplace culture based in empathy leads to better morale among workers. When people feel supported emotionally, they are more likely to approach challenges happily rather than feeling overwhelmed or disengaged.

Example: Leaders who celebrate individual successes publicly add to a positive atmosphere where workers feel recognized for their contributions.

Promoting Inclusivity: Empathetic leaders are more attuned to the diverse needs of their teams, allowing them to build inclusive environments where everyone feels welcome and valued.

Impact Analysis: Organizations that value inclusivity through empathetic practices report higher employee satisfaction rates as well as better performance outcomes due to diverse views being integrated into decision-making processes.

Encouraging Innovation: Teams led by empathetic leaders are often more creative because individuals feel safe taking risks without fear of failure or ridicule. This psychological safety supports creative thought and out-of-the-box solutions.

Research Insight: Companies known for fostering innovation often mention empathy as a key driver behind their success in developing groundbreaking goods or services.

Enhancing Emotional Intelligence (EQ): Leaders who practice empathy create greater emotional intelligence themselves—an important skill for navigating complex workplace dynamics successfully.

Impact Analysis: High EQ correlates with improved leadership effectiveness; leaders who understand both their own feelings and those of others can respond thoughtfully in various situations.

Inspiring and engaging your team through empathy is not just a leadership style; it is a powerful method that drives real results within organizations. By understanding empathy's role in successful communication, exploring how it can revolutionize your leadership approach, and recognizing its benefits on team relationships and overall morale, you can foster an environment where employees feel valued, supported, and motivated.

As you continue your journey through "Mastering Effective Communication for Leaders," remember that empathy is not merely an added benefit—it is a necessary ingredient for effective leadership in today's workplace setting. By embracing empathy as a core value within your leadership practice, you will unlock your team's full potential while producing collective success through connection, understanding, and shared purpose.

Techniques for Empathetic Communication

In "Mastering Effective Communication for Leaders: Unlocking the Secrets to Inspire and Engage Your Team," we dig into the important techniques for empathetic communication, a vital skill that can change leadership and team dynamics. Studies show that empathetic leaders have teams with 50% higher engagement levels, underscoring the importance of integrating empathy into daily interactions. This chapter will provide actionable insights for incorporating empathy into your communication style, methods for noticing and validating team members' feelings, and strategies to balance empathy with assertiveness when necessary.

Integrating Empathy into Daily Interactions

Empathy should not be an occasional practice; it must be woven into the fabric of daily meetings. Here are several actionable insights for leaders trying to improve their empathetic communication:

Practice Active Listening: Active listening is at the heart of empathetic communication. It includes fully concentrating on what is being said rather than just passively hearing the word. This means giving your full attention to the speaker, avoiding distractions, and showing that you are involved.

Action Step: When a team member talks, keep eye contact, nod in acknowledgment, and refrain from interrupting. After they stop speaking, paraphrase their message to prove understanding. For example, "So what I hear you saying is that you're feeling overwhelmed by your workload?"

Ask Open-Ended Questions: Encourage deeper talks by asking open-ended questions that invite team members to share their thoughts and feelings more easily. This way shows that you are genuinely interested in understanding their perspectives.

Action Step: Instead of asking yes-or-no questions, try questions like "What challenges are you facing right now?" or "How do you feel about the present project?" This invites more comprehensive responses and fosters a richer dialogue.

Validate feelings: Acknowledging and validating the feelings of your team members is crucial for sensitive communication. When someone shares their feelings, it's important to accept those emotions as legitimate.

Action Step: Use phrases like "I can see that this situation is frustrating for you" or "It's understandable to feel anxious about upcoming deadlines." This validation helps people feel heard and valued.

Share Personal Experiences: Sharing your own experiences can build a sense of connection and show empathy. When suitable, relate personal stories that resonate with what the other person is feeling.

Action Step: If a team member is struggling with a project, you might say, "I remember when I faced a similar challenge; it was tough but ultimately helped me grow." This sharing can foster trust and openness.

Be Mindful of Non-Verbal Cues: Non-verbal communication often expresses more than words alone. Pay attention to body language, facial expressions, and tone of voice when engaging with others.

Action Step: Ensure your non-verbal cues match with your message. For instance, if you're discussing a sensitive topic, keep an open posture and use a calm tone to express support and understanding.

Recognizing and Validating Team Members' Emotions

Understanding how to spot and validate the emotions of team members is important for fostering an empathetic workplace culture. Here are some techniques:

Observe Non-Verbal Signals: Team members may share their feelings through body language or facial expressions even when they don't directly voice them. Being attuned to these cues can help you spot when someone may need support.

Action Step: If you notice a coworker looking withdrawn or anxious during a meeting, consider checking in with them later to see how they're feeling.

Encourage Expression of Feelings: Create an atmosphere where team members feel safe expressing their feelings freely. Encourage them to share how they feel about projects or office relationships.

Action Step: During team meetings, invite people to share their thoughts on how they're feeling about current work or any challenges they face. You might say, "I'd like to hear how everyone is feeling about our current project."

Use Reflective Listening: Reflective listening includes restating what someone has said while acknowledging their feelings. This way shows that you are engaged and understand their feelings.

Action Step: If a team member shares that they are stressed about deadlines, reply with something like, "It sounds like you're feeling overwhelmed by the upcoming deadlines; let's discuss how we can manage this together."

Create Safe Spaces for Sharing: Establish regular check-ins or one-on-one talks where team members can share their thoughts in a safe environment without fear of judgment.

Action Step: Schedule informal coffee chats or feedback sessions where workers can share their thoughts freely in a relaxed setting.

MASTERING EFFECTIVE COMMUNICATION FOR LEADERS

Follow Up on Emotional Conversations: After discussing sensitive issues or feelings with a team member, follow up later to show that you care about their well-being.

Action Step: If someone shared that they were feeling stressed during a meeting last week, check in with them later by asking how they're doing now or if there's anything further they need help with.

Balancing Empathy with Assertiveness

While empathy is crucial in leadership communication, it's equally important to match it with assertiveness when appropriate. Here are ways for achieving this balance:

Use "I" Statements: When addressing problems or giving feedback, use "I" statements to express your feelings while having respect for the other person's view.

Action Step: Instead of saying, "You need to improve your performance," try saying, "I'm concerned about our project timelines and would like to discuss how we can work together to improve this." This method conveys your concerns without sounding accusatory.

Set Clear Boundaries: While being empathetic is important, leaders must also set boundaries to ensure that standards are clear and respected.

Action Step: Communicate clearly what behaviors are accepted and what consequences may arise if those limits are crossed. For example, if someone regularly misses deadlines despite the support offered, address it directly while still showing concern for their position.

Be Honest About flaws: Sometimes showing empathy means admitting your flaws as a leader. Be honest about what you can truly provide in terms of help or resources.

MASTERING EFFECTIVE COMMUNICATION FOR LEADERS

Action Step: If an employee asks for additional resources that aren't feasible within budget constraints, explain this clearly while showing understanding of their needs—"I understand that having more resources would help; however, we currently have budget limitations we must adhere to."

Encourage Accountability: While empathizing with team members' challenges is important, leaders should also encourage accountability for actions taken within the workplace setting.

Action Step: When discussing performance issues empathetically but assertively state expectations moving forward—"I appreciate your efforts during this busy period; however, I need us all to meet our deadlines consistently."

Practice Assertive Communication Techniques: Employ assertive communication techniques such as keeping eye contact and using confident body language while talking sensitive topics empathetically.

Action Step: When addressing a problem with a team member who may be suffering emotionally but needs constructive feedback as well—maintain composure while showing concern—"I want to support you through this challenge; however, we need to address how we can improve our outcomes together."

Techniques for empathetic communication are important tools for leaders looking to inspire and engage their teams effectively. By integrating empathy into daily interactions through active listening, recognizing emotions, validating experiences, and balancing empathy with assertiveness, leaders can create an environment where team members feel valued and understood.

MASTERING EFFECTIVE COMMUNICATION FOR LEADERS

As you continue your journey through "Mastering Effective Communication for Leaders," remember that empathy is not merely an emotional reaction; it is a strategic method that improves relationships within teams while driving performance improvement across organizations. By embracing these techniques fully in your leadership practice, you will cultivate stronger connections with your team members—ultimately fostering collaboration, innovation, and success within your company.

Celebrating Team Achievements

In "Mastering Effective Communication for Leaders: Unlocking the Secrets to Inspire and Engage Your Team," the value of recognizing and celebrating wins within your team cannot be overstated. Studies suggest that teams with a culture of recognition have significantly higher engagement levels, leading to better performance and morale. This chapter will uncover the importance of celebrating team achievements, explore various ways to recognize contributions and discuss how public recognition creates a culture of appreciation that inspires continued excellence.

3.2 Importance Of Recognizing And Celebrating Successes

Celebrating team success is important for several reasons:

Boosting Morale: Acknowledging achievements, whether big or small, boosts team morale. When employees feel appreciated for their hard work, they are more likely to stay motivated and committed to their jobs.

Example: A simple "thank you" or recognition during a team meeting can greatly enhance an employee's sense of belonging and worth within the company.

Encouraging Continued Efforts: Celebrations serve as positive reinforcement that pushes workers to continue aiming for excellence. When team members see that their efforts lead to praise, they are more likely to keep high-performance levels.

Research Insight: According to a study by Gallup, companies that prioritize employee recognition have 14% better productivity than those that do not.

Fostering Team Cohesion: Celebrating wins together improves relationships among team members. Shared celebrations build bonding experiences that improve collaboration and teamwork.

Example: Organizing a team lunch or outing after finishing a project can foster camaraderie and reinforce the idea that everyone added to the success.

Creating a Positive Work Culture: Regularly recognizing successes adds to a positive workplace culture where workers feel valued and respected. This culture draws talent and keeps top performers.

Impact Analysis: Companies with strong recognition programs report lower turnover rates and better employee satisfaction scores, showing the long-term benefits of celebrating wins.

Setting a Precedent for Future Success: Celebrating achievements sets benchmarks for what success looks like within the company. It sets standards for future success and encourages employees to aim for similar accomplishments.

Example: When a team completes a tough project, recognizing their efforts not only acknowledges their hard work but also sets a standard for future projects.

Different Ways To Acknowledge Contributions

There are numerous ways leaders can recognize efforts within their teams. Here are some fast methods:

Public Recognition: Recognizing achievements publicly during meetings or through company-wide messages can amplify the effect of acknowledgment. Public praise supports the value of the individual's efforts.

Action Step: Create a "shout-out" segment in team meetings where members can recognize each other's wins. This practice helps peer-to-peer recognition and builds a supportive environment.

Personalized Thank-You Notes: A handwritten note expressing thanks can make a significant effect on an employee's morale. Personalization shows that you respect their specific efforts.

Action Step: After completing a project, take time to write personalized thank-you notes to team members highlighting what they did well and how it added to the general success.

Celebration Events: Organizing events such as parties or team outings can create memorable experiences focused around celebrating successes.

These events support team bonding while acknowledging hard work.

Action Step: Plan quarterly celebrations where the entire team can meet to celebrate milestones made during that time, such as successful project completions or sales targets met.

Social Media Recognition: Sharing successes on social media platforms shows your team's accomplishments beyond the company while enhancing visibility and pride among workers.

Action Step: Post about team successes on platforms like LinkedIn or Twitter, tagging important individuals and highlighting their contributions to foster a feeling of pride in their work.

Awards and Incentives: Implementing formal recognition programs with awards or incentives can urge workers to try for excellence. These programs can include "Employee of the Month" awards or success bonuses.

Action Step: Create criteria for awards based on specific behaviors or successes that fit with organizational values, ensuring that recognition is meaningful and tied to desired outcomes.

3.3 The Impact Of Public Recognition On Team Dynamics

Public recognition plays a vital part in creating a culture of appreciation within teams. Here are some key impacts:

Enhancing Visibility: Publicly recognizing achievements guarantees that accomplishments do not go unnoticed within the company. This exposure supports the idea that hard work is valued at all levels.

Impact Analysis: Employees who feel appreciated are 63% more likely to say they will stay at their job for at least another year compared to those who do not receive recognition.

Encouraging Peer Recognition: When leaders practice public acknowledgment, it pushes others within the team to recognize each other's contributions as well, creating an environment where appreciation becomes part of the culture.

Example: A leader who regularly acknowledges team members' efforts publicly sets an example for others, fostering an atmosphere where peer-to-peer recognition flourishes.

Building Confidence and Self-Esteem: Public recognition boosts individuals' confidence and self-esteem, reinforcing their belief in their skills and contributions to the team's success.

Impact Analysis: Employees who receive public recognition report feeling more confident in their roles, which translates into better productivity and engagement levels at work.

Strengthening Team Bonds: Celebrating successes together enhances relationships among team members by building shared experiences focused around achievement, fostering collaboration and teamwork.

Example: When teams enjoy milestones together—whether through social events or public acknowledgment—they strengthen their bonds, making it easier to work on future projects.

Inspiring Continued Excellence: Publicly recognizing successes serves as motivation for others within the company to aim for similar accomplishments, creating an environment focused on excellence.

Research Insight: According to research from O.C. Tanner Institute, organizations that value employee recognition see 31% lower voluntary turnover rates—demonstrating how public acknowledgment inspires ongoing commitment from workers.

Celebrating team achievements is not merely an act of acknowledgment; it is a strategic method that enhances morale, fosters teamwork, and drives business success. By recognizing successes—both big and small—leaders create an environment where workers feel valued, driven, and engaged in their work.

As you continue your journey through "Mastering Effective Communication for Leaders," remember that celebrating achievements is important for building strong teams and creating a positive workplace culture. By adopting various methods of acknowledgment and embracing public recognition as part of your leadership practice, you will inspire your team members toward continued greatness while reinforcing the importance of collective success within your organization.

MASTERING EFFECTIVE COMMUNICATION FOR LEADERS

CONCLUSION

In "Mastering Effective Communication for Leaders: Unlocking the Secrets to Inspire and Engage Your Team," we have explored the essential components of effective communication that enable leaders to inspire, engage, and drive their teams toward collective success. Throughout this journey, we have highlighted the significance of empathy, active listening, clarity, and recognition in creating a positive work environment. As we end this study, it is crucial to summarize the key insights from each chapter, reinforcing the idea that mastering effective communication is an ongoing journey.

Summary of Key Insights

The Foundations of Effective Leadership Communication: We began by emphasizing the value of clarity and conciseness in communication. Clear messaging helps align team efforts with corporate goals, reduces misunderstandings, and

MASTERING EFFECTIVE COMMUNICATION FOR LEADERS

improves decision-making. By avoiding jargon and ambiguity, leaders can promote trust and collaboration within their teams. The foundation of successful communication lies in establishing transparency and honesty, which are critical for building strong relationships and ensuring that team members feel valued.

Active Listening: The next chapter focused on the role of active listening in building good relationships. Active listening includes fully engaging with team members, acknowledging their feelings, and responding thoughtfully. This practice not only enhances understanding but also fosters a setting where employees feel safe to express their concerns. By implementing strategies such as undivided attention, reflective listening, and open-ended questioning, leaders can create an atmosphere of open dialogue that supports collaboration and innovation.

Navigating Challenging Conversations: We then studied techniques for navigating difficult discussions while keeping team morale. Identifying the right time and place for tough conversations is important for effective communication. Leaders must frame issues constructively and create a solution-focused mindset to support collaboration during conflicts. By addressing challenges promptly and fostering an environment of trust, leaders can guide their teams through difficult talks toward positive results.

Techniques for Empathetic Communication: Empathy emerged as a transformative factor in leadership communication. We covered actionable ideas for integrating empathy into daily interactions, recognizing and validating team members' emotions, and balancing empathy with assertiveness when necessary. Empathetic leaders create an environment where workers feel understood and valued, enhancing motivation and

MASTERING EFFECTIVE COMMUNICATION FOR LEADERS

engagement while fostering strong relationships within the team.

Celebrating Team Achievements: Finally, we explored the importance of recognizing and celebrating successes within teams. Celebrating achievements boosts morale, encourages continued efforts, builds team cohesion, and creates a positive work atmosphere. Leaders can recognize contributions through public recognition, personalized thank-you notes, celebration events, social media recognition, and awards or incentives. Public recognition not only improves visibility but also inspires ongoing commitment to excellence among team members.

The Ongoing Journey of Mastering Effective Communication

Mastering effective communication is not a one-time achievement; it is an ongoing journey that needs continuous learning and practice. As leaders navigate the complexities of their roles, they must stay committed to honing their communication skills to inspire their teams successfully.

Consistency is Key: Consistently applying the principles outlined in this book will lead to a lasting impact within your company. Regularly practicing active listening, empathetic communication, clear articulation of goals, and recognizing successes will reinforce a culture of trust and cooperation.

Seek Feedback: Encourage feedback from your team regarding your communication style and success. This openness not only demonstrates humility but also offers valuable insights into areas for improvement.

Adaptability: Recognize that different situations may require different communication methods. Be flexible in your style to accommodate the diverse needs of your team members while staying true to your authentic leadership voice.

Continuous Learning: Stay informed about new communication strategies and methods through workshops, seminars, or reading materials focused on leadership development. The landscape of effective communication is ever-evolving; keeping current will enhance your effectiveness as a leader.

Encouragement for Application

As you reflect on the insights shared throughout this book, I encourage you to adopt these principles consistently in your leadership practices. Embrace the power of empathetic conversation to connect with your team on a deeper level. Foster an atmosphere where open dialogue thrives, where achievements are celebrated regularly, and where every team member feels valued.

By committing to these practices, you will not only enhance your leadership effectiveness but also inspire those around you to engage fully in their roles—ultimately moving your organization toward greater success through collective effort and shared understanding.

In conclusion, remember that effective communication is not just about conveying messages; it's about building relationships that enable individuals to excel together as a cohesive unit. As you start on this journey of mastering effective communication in leadership, may you inspire others to reach new heights while creating an environment where everyone feels empowered to contribute their best efforts toward shared goals.

Thank you so much for making it to the end of the book!

I truly appreciate the time you've taken to read my work. As an independent Kindle publisher, your support means everything to me. I hope you've found valuable and useful insights in these pages.

If you could spare just 60 seconds, I'd love to hear your honest feedback on Amazon. Your feedback makes a huge difference and it does wonders for the book. I also enjoy hearing about your experiences with it!

To leave your feedback, simply copy the link below and paste it into your browser:

www.ingramcontent.com/pod-product-compliance
Lightning Source LLC
Chambersburg PA
CBHW071652240526
45469CB00021B/2264